Intellectual Property Rights and International Receipts of Royalties and Licensing Fees

David Riker

U.S. International Trade Commission, Office of Economics, Research Division [1]

08-26-14

I0393907

Abstract

This paper measures the strength of intellectual property rights in different countries using an econometric model of U.S. cross-border receipts of royalties and license fees. The econometric estimates are correlated with country indices of intellectual property rights in the literature, but they are more comprehensive, detailed, and up-to-date than alternative indices.

Keywords: intellectual property rights, international trade in services, econometric analysis

JEL Codes: C5, F14, O34

1. Introduction

It is important, but difficult, to measure the strength of intellectual property rights (IPRs) in different countries. It is important because the protection of IPRs can contribute significantly to a country's economic performance. It can affect the country's productivity, ability to attract inward foreign direct investment, incentives to innovate, consumer prices and aggregate economic growth.[2] A country's protection of IPRs can also contribute to the economic performance of its trading partners. They benefit from expanded markets for their products and royalty and licensing fees from the use of their technologies.[3]

---

[1] This working paper is the result of ongoing professional research of ITC Staff and is solely meant to represent the opinions and professional research of the author. It is not meant to represent in any way the views of the U.S. International Trade Commission or any of its individual Commissioners. Please address any correspondence to David.Riker@usitc.gov.

[2] For example, Branstetter and Saggi (2012) models the impact of IPRs on foreign direct investment, employment, and real wages in a country.

[3] For example, Ivus (2010) and Riker (2012) are econometric estimates of the impact of IPRs on international trade flows. Qiu and Yu (2010) provide econometric evidence that innovation in developed countries responded positively to IPR reforms in their trade partners.

1

It is difficult to measure the strength of IPRs in different countries because intellectual property consists of many different types of intangible assets and many different types of policies, including patents, copyrights, and protection of trademarks, trade secrets, industrial designs, and plant varieties.[4] It is difficult to assess how strictly the laws and rules on the books are enforced and to quantify their economic significance.[5]

Section 2 in this paper discusses several indices of the protection of IPRs that are currently available in the literature. These include an indicator of intellectual property protection in the *Global Competitiveness Report* of the World Economic Forum (WEF), an index of patent protection in Park (2008), and country-specific software piracy rates published by the Business Software Alliance.

Sections 3 through 6 develop a new econometric measure of the strength of IPRs in 33 countries based on data on U.S. cross-border receipts of international royalties and license fees (RLF) receipts. Section 3 presents the economic modeling framework and the econometric specification. RLF receipts are modeled as a function of factors that determine a country's IPR protection and other factors that directly affect the country's RLF receipts for a given IPR regime. Section 4 discusses the data sources, and Section 5 reports the econometric estimates for different types of intellectual property assets and sensitivity analyses that include alternative estimation techniques.

This paper contributes to the literature on multi-country studies of IPRs by providing indices that are more detailed, more comprehensive, and more up-to-date than alternatives in the literature. The indices are estimated separately for specific types of intellectual property assets (industrial processes, software, films and trademarks) and also for a combination of all asset types. Since the models infer the level of IPR protection based on its effect on RLF receipts, the models measure the market relevance of the IPRs.

There are several econometric studies in the literature that estimate the *impact* of IPRs on international RLF receipts and trade. These studies are certainly related, but they do not measure the *level of IPR protection* in the countries. Instead, the studies adopt a published index or other data on IPR reforms, which they treat as an exogenous determinant of international trade, cross-border royalties and licensing, or foreign direct investment. For example, Branstetter, Fisman, and Foley (2006) provide firm-

---

[4] Maskus (2000) provides a detailed description of the different types of intellectual property and the policies developed to protect them.

[5] Even when the laws and rules are strictly enforced they might not be economically relevant. For example, a country might grant extensive patent protection for products that are not commercially viable.

level econometric evidence that foreign affiliates of patent-intensive U.S. parent companies paid significantly higher royalties and licensing fees due to patent reforms in the countries that hosted their foreign affiliates.[6]

Section 6 compares the different indices. It reports rank correlations between the model-based indices and the World Economic Forum, Business Software Alliance, and Park indices in Section 2. Section 7 provides concluding remarks.

2. Indices of Intellectual Property Protection in the Literature

Table 1 offers a side-by-side comparison of three indicators of the strength of IPR protection in 33 countries. The first indicator is an index of intellectual property protection from the WEF's *Global Competitiveness Report* for 2012-2013.[7] The indicator is based on WEF's Executive Opinion Survey. It measures market participants' perceptions about the effectiveness of policies in place. The WEF index ranges from 1 (very weak) to 7 (very strong). It is a general index of IPRs that does not specifically focus on patent protection or on copyrights. The WEF measure for 2011-2012 is available for 144 countries.

The second indicator in Table 1 is an index of patent protection from Park (2008). This index and its predecessor in Ginarte and Park (1997) are commonly used in studies of the economic effects of IPRs.[8] The Park index for 2005 is available for 122 countries and is focused exclusively on patents. The index is an average of the countries' scores on five dimensions: the strength of patent coverage, membership in international treaties, duration of patent coverage, enforcement mechanisms and restrictions.

The third indicator in Table 1 is the 2011 software piracy rates in Business Software Alliance (2012). The piracy rates are reported for 111 countries based on a survey of approximately 15,000 computer users around the world. The measure is specific to software.

The Global Intellectual Property Center (GIPC) at the U.S. Chamber of Commerce also publishes an international index of IPRs for 25 countries. It is based on the countries' scores on 30 indicators that cover patents, copyrights, trademarks, trade secrets, enforcement and ratification of international treaties. GIPC's scoring is based on data compiled from many different sources. Since the GIPC index covers only half of the 33 countries in Table 1, it is not included in the comparison.

---

[6] Park and Lippoldt (2005) is another excellent example.

[7] Specifically, it is Indicator 1.02 in WEF's *Global Competitiveness Index*.

[8] Examples of studies that use the Park index include Maskus (2000), Ivus (2010), Chu and Peng (2011), Chu, Cozzi and Galli (2012), Park (2012) and Bilir (2014).

3

3. Model of U.S. Royalty Receipts

This section presents the conceptual framework and the econometric specification. If intellectual property is protected in the foreign market, then IPRs might generate U.S. RLF receipts, though there is some ambiguity. Stronger protection of IPRs in a foreign market might increase a U.S. firm's willingness to license its technology to foreign producers, including its own foreign affiliates. On the other hand, stronger IPRs might stimulate innovation in competing local producers. The value of RLF receipts is likely increasing in the economic size of the foreign market. RLF receipts are likely decreasing in distance, which generally limits international economic interactions including licensing of technologies. They are also likely decreasing in the country's corporate tax rate, reflecting efforts by multinational firms to lower their global tax burdens. If the intellectual property is not protected, then the country's expenditures on the same products would go to non-protected local, American, or third-country producers, but in any case there would not generate significant U.S. RLF receipts.

Equation (1) is a log-linear model that relates these economic variables.

$$rlf_{act} = y_{ct} + \beta_a\, ipr_{ct} + \gamma_a\, dist_c + \delta_a\, tx_{ct} + \theta_a + \epsilon_{act} \tag{1}$$

The variable rlf_{act} represents the log of U.S. cross-border RLFs for asset type a from country c in year t, y_{ct} is the log of the GDP of country c in year t, and ipr_{act} represents a measure of the strength of IPR protection for asset type a in country c in year t.[9] The variable tx_{ct} is the log of the corporate tax rate in country c in year t. The model includes asset type fixed effects that control for differences in the expenditure shares of the asset types and also for differences in U.S. technological capability in each of the types.

The level of IPR protection for asset type a in country c in year t is a latent variable that depends on several observable country characteristics, as in equation (2).

$$ipr_{act} = \kappa_a\, col_c + \lambda_a\, gdppc_{ct} + \rho_a\, fta_{ct} \tag{2}$$

The variable col_c is a binary variable that indicates whether country c was part of the former colonial systems of the United Kingdom or France.[10] The variable $gdppc_{ct}$ is the log of real GDP per capita in country c in year t, a conventional measure of a country's level of economic development. The variable

---

[9] For example, software and trademarks are different asset types.

[10] Ivus (2010) finds that this variable is a significant determinant of IPR reforms.

fta_{ct} is a binary variable that indicates whether country c has an FTA with the United States in year t that includes intellectual property provisions.

The premise of the econometric analysis is that ipr_{act} is unobserved, and that equation (2) identifies a set of economic factors that affect ipr_{act} but do not enter equation (1) except through their effect on ipr_{act}. The reduced-form model in equation (3) is derived by substituting equation (2) into equation (1).

$$r_{act} = \beta_a \kappa_a\, col_c + \beta_a \lambda_a\, gdppc_{ct} + \beta_a \rho_a\, fta_{ct} + \gamma_a\, dist_c + \delta_a\, tx_{ct} + \theta_a + \epsilon_{act} \tag{3}$$

The variable r_{act} is the log of U.S. RLF receipts as a share of the GDP of the country, or $rlf_{act} - y_{ct}$. By projecting r_{act} onto the determinants of ipr_{act} and other covariates, the specification in equation (3) estimates the linear combination of the variables in equation (2) that best fits the data on RLF receipts. In this way, the model estimates an index of IPR protection for each asset type, country, and year. After estimating the regression coefficients $\beta_a \kappa_a$, $\beta_a \lambda_a$ and $\beta_a \rho_a$ using equation (3), the value of $index_{act}$ for each asset type and country in 2012 is calculated using equation (4).

$$index_{act} = \beta_a \kappa_a\, col_c + \beta_a \lambda_a\, gdppc_{ct} + \beta_a \rho_a\, fta_{ct} \tag{4}$$

The variable $index_{act}$ provides a relative measure of IPR protection in country c, within asset type a and year t. It does not separate the impact of IPRs on RLF receipts, i.e., β_a, from the effect of the three variables on ipr_{act}. Isolating β_a would require a reliable direct measure of IPRs. However, the value of β_a is not needed to calculate the ratio of the index values for countries c and c', $index_{act}/index_{ac't}$, and so it is not needed to generate a ranking of the countries' protection of IPRs.

4. Data

The data on U.S. cross-border RLF receipts are from the U.S. Bureau of Economic Analysis (BEA). RLF receipts are reported in Table 4a of BEA's International Services Database in current dollars by year, source country and type of intangible asset. In 2012, total RLF receipts accounted for 19.8 percent of all U.S. receipts for cross-border exports of private services.[11] This is down slightly from 20.7 percent in 2006.

The econometric model focuses on U.S. RLF receipts from 33 of the 34 individual countries that are reported in the BEA database. The model does not include the data for Bermuda, because the values

---

[11] BEA, *U.S. International Services Database, Detailed Statistics for Cross-Border Trade*, Table 1a. Grimm and Sharma (2013) provides a complete overview of the recent BEA data.

are missing for most asset types. Together, the 33 countries accounted for 91 percent of total U.S. RLF receipts in 2012.

Table 2 reports the 2006 and 2012 value of U.S. RLF receipts for the eight types of assets that are reported by BEA. The eight types are industrial processes; books, records, and tapes; film and television tape distribution; broadcasting and recording of live events; franchise fees; trademarks; and other intangibles. RLF receipts for industrial processes have the largest dollar value in both years, followed by general use computer software. Film and television tape distribution and trademarks also account for an economically significant share of total RLF receipts. The four largest types together account for 93 percent of total RLF receipts in 2012.

Table 3 reports the value of RLF receipts by source country in 2006 and 2012, in current U.S. dollars and as a share of the source country's GDP. In terms of dollar values, Ireland, Japan, Canada, and the United Kingdom sent the largest RLF payments to the United States in 2012. As a share of the source country's GDP, Ireland, Singapore, Switzerland, and Taiwan sent the largest RLF payments.

The econometric model utilizes data from several other sources. The data on GDP and GDP per capita are from the International Monetary Fund's *World Economic Outlook* database.[12] The corporate tax rates for the 33 countries are from KPMG.[13] The data on colonial ties are from the CIA Fact Book.[14] The data on international distances are from CEPII.[15]

Table 4 reports several country characteristics that are correlated with RLF receipts and with the country's protection of IPRs. The first column reports U.S. RLF receipts as a share of the GDP of the foreign country. The variables in the next two columns are determinants of RLF receipts that are probably independent of the country's protection of IPRs. There is a negative correlation between the RLF shares and the corporate tax rate (-0.55) and a weaker negative correlation between these shares and international distance (-0.14). The variables in the three final columns are factors that determine the strength of the country's protection of IPRs: the level of economic development, whether the source country was part of the former colonial systems of the United Kingdom or France, and whether the country has an FTA with the United States that includes intellectual property provisions.

---

[12] These data are publicly available at http://www.imf.org/external/ns/cs.aspx?id=28.

[13] These data are publicly available at http://www.kpmg.com/global/en/services/tax/tax-tools-and-resources/pages/corporate-tax-rates-tables.aspx. (Accessed 6/23/14).

[14] These data are publicly available at https://www.cia.gov/cia/publications/factbook/index.html.

[15] These data are publicly available at http://www.cepii.com/CEPII/en/bdd_modele/bdd.asp.

The BEA dataset is missing values for some asset types, countries and years. Overall, 6.25 percent of the country-asset-year values are not disclosed in the public BEA data. RLF receipts were imputed for the non-disclosure cells. The first step of the imputation was to calculate the total missing value for each country-year by subtracting the sum of the non-missing amounts from the reported total RLF receipts for the country-year. The second step was to allocate this total missing value for each country and year across the cells that were missing values in proportion to the overall relative shares of each of the asset types in BEA's dataset.

5. Econometric Estimation

The first set of regressions estimate the coefficients of the model in equation (4) using OLS and the imputations described above. These coefficient estimates are reported in the first column of Table 5. The first four explanatory variables are mostly statistically significant and have the expected signs. One exception is the estimated coefficient on corporate tax rates for films. The other exception is the coefficient on colonial ties for trademarks; it has the expected sign, but it is not significantly different from zero. The model in the first column pools all of the asset types together and includes asset fixed effects. The largest fixed effect is for industrial processes. The smallest fixed effect is for broadcasting and recording of live events. The fifth explanatory variable, the indicator for whether the country has an FTA with intellectual property provisions, is positive and statistically significant for the pooled estimates and for software but is not statistically significant for the other individual asset types.

Table 6 reports point estimates for the index of IPR protection for each of the 33 countries. They are calculated using the coefficient estimates in the first column of Table 5 and the 2012 values for the variables on the right-hand side of equation (2). The table also reports 95% confidence intervals for each point estimate.[16] The five countries with the highest index values are Australia, Singapore, Canada, Ireland and France. The five countries with the lowest index values are the Philippines, Indonesia, India, Thailand and China.

Table 7 repeats the point estimates for the index that pools together all of the asset types (for the sake of comparison) and adds indices for each of the four largest types, based on the coefficient estimates in the corresponding columns in Table 5. The ranking of countries varies a little across the different asset types. For example, Switzerland, Chile and Mexico are ranked lower for industrial processes than they are in the pooled ranking. Chile, Malaysia and India are ranked higher for software than they are in the pooled ranking.

---

[16] To reduce the size of the tables, the rest of the tables in this paper only report point estimates.

Table 8 applies an alternative estimation technique to the data. The table repeats the estimates of the coefficients from the OLS model that pools all of the asset types (for the sake of comparison) and adds estimates from a Poisson model.[17] The point estimates are very similar for the two estimators. The largest differences are the coefficients on the corporate tax rate and the FTA indicator. Table 9 reports the index values for the two models in Table 8. The index values are different in magnitude, but the country rankings are similar across the two columns, with a few exceptions. Sweden, Malaysia, Taiwan and Thailand drops in rank when the index is based on the Poisson model. The estimates suggest that the country rankings in Table 6 are not especially sensitive to the estimation technique.

The next variation excludes observations with imputed values. Table 10 repeats the OLS model that pools all of the types of assets and includes imputed values, and then it adds an OLS pooled model without the imputed values. Excluding the observations with imputed values reduces the size of the estimation sample from 1,724 observations to 1,595. The only notable difference between the two sets of coefficient estimates is the coefficient on the log of the corporate tax rate.

The final sensitivity analysis adds year fixed effects to the econometric specification. In theory, these effects could control for the stock of innovative technologies and creative works owned by the United States, which varies over time but are common among the countries that license the intellectual property. The final column in Table 10 reports the estimated coefficients on all of the explanatory variables (except the year fixed effects). The year fixed effects are not statistically significant at the 5% level, either jointly or individually.[18]

6. Rank Correlations of the Indices

Table 11 compares the different indices. The top panel of the table reports Spearman rank correlations for the three indices of IPR protection from the literature. The WEF and BSA indices are moderately correlated with each other, while the Park index is relatively distinct. This is not surprising, since the Park index is calculated for an earlier year.[19] Also, the Park index is specific to patents. It is not a general measure of intellectual property protection like the WEF index.

---

[17] Santos Silva and Tenreyro (2006, 2011) recommend using a Poisson estimator to model international trade flows, in order to address heterogeneity in the data and zero values for some of the country pairs.

[18] In the Wald test that the coefficients on the year fixed effects are jointly different from zero, the value of the F statistic is 0.78 and the p-value is 0.5850.

[19] The most recent year of the Park index is 2005, while the two other indices are for 2011.

The bottom panel in Table 11 reports Spearman rank correlations between the indices based on the econometric model (in Table 7 and 9) and the three indices from the literature. The asset-specific indices for industrial processes and films have the highest correlations with the indices in the literature, and the indices for software and trademarks have the lowest. Among the three indices based on the models that pools together all of the asset types, the index calculated from the Poisson model has a relatively high correlation with the WEF index and the non-piracy rate based on the BSA data.

7. Conclusions

The rankings of countries' IPR protection based on the econometric models are similar to other indices in the literature. Singapore, Switzerland, and the United Kingdom are at or near the top along with most of the advanced countries, while India and Indonesia are near the bottom along with most of the developing countries. However, the indices based on the econometric models have several advantages: they can be updated with the latest BEA data on RLF receipts, and they provide information by asset type and also for all asset types combined.

References

Bilar, L.K. (2014): "Patent Laws, Product-Cycle Lengths, and Multinational Activity." *American Economic Review* 104(7): 1979-2013.

Branstetter, L., R. Fisman, and C. Foley (2006): "Do Stronger Intellectual Property Rights Increase International Technology Transfer? Empirical Evidence from U.S. Firm-Level Panel Data." Quarterly Journal of Economics 2 (1): 321-349.

Branstetter, L. and K. Saggi (2012): "Intellectual Property Rights, Foreign Direct Investment, and Industrial Development." *Economic Journal* 121:1161-1191.

Business Software Alliance (2012): *Shadow Market: 2011 BSA Global Software Piracy Study, Ninth Edition.* http://globalstudy.bsa.org/2011/ (Accessed 6/25/14).

Chu, A.C., G. Cozzi, and S. Galli (2012): "Does Intellectual Monopoly Stimulate or Stifle Innovation." *European Economic Review* 56: 727-746.

Chu, A.C. and S.K. Peng (2011): "International Intellectual Property Rights: Effects on Growth, Welfare and Income Inequality." *Journal of Macroeconomics* 33: 276-287.

Ginarte, J. and W. Park (1997): "Determinants of Patent Rights: A Cross-National Study." *Research Policy* 26: 283-301.

Grimm, A. and C. Sharma (2013): "U.S. International Services: Cross-Border Trade in 2012 and Services Supplied Through Affiliates in 2011." *Survey of Current Business*, October, 25-41.

Ivus, O. (2010): "Do Stronger Patent Rights Raise High-Tech Exports to the Developing World?" *Journal of International Economics* 81: 38-47.

Qiu, L. and H. Yu (2010): "Does the Protection of Foreign Intellectual Property Stimulate Innovation in the US?" *Review of International Economics* 18(5): 882-895.

Park, W. (2008): "International Patent Protection: 1960-2005." *Research Policy* 37: 761-766.

Park, W. and D. Lippoldt (2005): "International Licensing and Strengthening of Intellectual Property Rights in Developing Countries During the 1990s." *OECD Economic Studies* 40: 7-48.

Riker, D. (2012): "Has Special 301 Promoted U.S. Manufacturing Exports?" *Review of International Economics* 20 (2): 288-298.

Santos Silva, J. and S. Tenreyro (2006): "The Log of Gravity." *Review of Economics and Statistics* 88(4): 641-658.

Santos Silva, J. and S. Tenreyro (2011): "Further Simulation Evidence on the Performance of the Poisson-PML Estimator." *Economics Letters* 112 (2): 220-222.

Schwab, K. (2012): *The Global Competitiveness Report 2012-2013: Full Data Edition*. Geneva: World Economic Forum.

U.S. Bureau of Economic Analysis (2014): U.S. International Services Database, *Detailed Statistics for Cross-Border Trade*, various tables. http://www.bea.gov/international/international_services.htm (Accessed 6/16/14).

U.S. Chamber of Commerce, Global Intellectual Property Center (2014): *Charting the Course: GIPC International IP Index*, Second Edition. (Accessed 6/20/14) At www.theglobalipcenter.com/wp-content/themes/gipc/map-index/assets/pdf/Index_Map_Index_**2ndEdition**.pdf.

Table 1: Measures of Intellectual Property Protection in the Literature

Countries	WEF Indicator 1.02 for 2011-2012	Park (2008) Index of Patent Protection for 2005	Business Software Alliance Software Piracy Rate for 2011
New Zealand	6.1	4.01	22
Singapore	6.1	4.21	33
Switzerland	6.0	4.33	25
Netherlands	5.9	4.67	27
United Kingdom	5.9	4.54	26
France	5.6	4.67	37
Germany	5.6	4.50	26
Hong Kong	5.6	3.81	43
Sweden	5.6	4.54	24
Ireland	5.5	4.67	34
Norway	5.5	4.17	27
Canada	5.4	4.67	27
Japan	5.4	4.67	21
Australia	5.3	4.17	23
South Africa	5.3	4.25	35
Belgium	5.2	4.67	24
Taiwan	5.2	3.74	37
Saudi Arabia	5.1	2.98	51
Malaysia	4.9	3.48	55
Israel	4.8	4.13	31
Korea	4.3	4.33	40
Spain	4.0	4.33	44
China	3.9	4.08	77
Chile	3.7	4.28	61
India	3.7	3.76	63
Indonesia	3.7	2.77	86
Italy	3.7	4.67	48
Brazil	3.5	3.59	53
Mexico	3.5	3.88	57
Philippines	3.2	4.18	70
Thailand	3.1	2.66	72
Argentina	2.4	3.98	69
Venezuela	1.7	3.32	88

Table 2: U.S. Cross-Border Royalty Receipts by Type (in Millions of Current U.S. Dollars)

Type of Asset	2006	2012
Industrial Processes	32,415	42,777
General Use Computer Software (Software)	22,655	39,544
Trademarks	10,383	16,808
Film and Television Tape Distribution (Films)	12,823	16,222
Franchise Fees	3,270	5,968
Books, Records, and Tapes (Books)	1,473	1,771
Broadcasting and Recording of Live Events	425	842
Other Intangibles	106	251
Total Royalties and License Fees	83,549	124,182

Source: BEA U.S. International Services Database, Detailed Statistics for Cross-Border Trade, Table 4a.

Table 3: U.S. Total Royalty and License Fee Receipts in 2006 and 2012

Country	Value of RLF Receipts in 2006 (in million USD)	Receipts as a Share if GDP in 2006 (in percent)	Value of RLF Receipts in 2012 (in million USD)	Receipts as a Share if GDP in 2012 (in percent)
Ireland	7,448	3.340	12,955	6.147
Japan	9,973	0.229	10,365	0.175
United Kingdom	10,654	0.428	9,771	0.393
Canada	7,280	0.555	9,818	0.539
Switzerland	6,559	1.619	9,303	1.474
Germany	5,910	0.203	6,339	0.185
Netherlands	1,780	0.003	5,811	0.754
Taiwan	1,538	0.409	5,750	1.210
Korea	2,602	0.273	5,456	0.483
Singapore	2,663	1.824	5,001	1.759
China	1,551	0.057	4,817	0.059
Brazil	1,514	0.139	3,680	0.164
Australia	2,035	0.260	3,357	0.216
France	3,593	0.159	3,264	0.125
Mexico	2,011	0.208	3,100	0.262
Belgium	1,303	0.325	2,380	0.493
Italy	2,024	0.108	1,671	0.083
Spain	1,626	0.131	1,446	0.109
Sweden	810	0.203	860	0.164
India	409	0.043	835	0.045
South Africa	497	0.002	807	0.211
Hong Kong	560	0.003	740	0.282
Argentina	320	0.151	733	0.154
Venezuela	297	0.162	665	0.174
Philippines	207	0.002	563	0.225
Malaysia	287	0.176	515	0.169
Thailand	239	1.115	489	0.134
Chile	172	0.001	469	0.176
Israel	173	0.115	424	0.165
Saudi Arabia	166	0.044	410	0.056
New Zealand	249	0.229	340	0.200
Indonesia	128	0.035	280	0.032
Norway	253	0.074	268	0.054
Rest of the World	6,718		11,501	

Note: The countries are sorted in descending order based on the value of RLF receipts in 2012.

14

Table 4: Country Characteristics in 2012

Country	RLF Receipts as a Share of GDP (in percent)	Corporate Tax Rate (in percent)	International Distance (kilometer)	British or French Colony	High Income Country	FTA with IPR Provisions
Ireland	6.147	12.50	5,456	Yes	Yes	No
Singapore	1.759	17.00	15,553	Yes	Yes	Yes
Switzerland	1.474	18.06	6,561	No	Yes	No
Taiwan	1.210	17.00	12,666	No	Yes	No
Netherlands	0.754	25.00	6,205	No	Yes	No
Canada	0.539	26.00	732	Yes	Yes	Yes
Belgium	0.493	33.99	6,232	No	Yes	No
Korea	0.483	24.20	11,189	No	Yes	Yes
United Kingdom	0.393	24.00	5,914	Yes	Yes	No
Hong Kong	0.282	16.50	13,129	No	Yes	No
Mexico	0.262	30.00	3,030	No	No	Yes
Philippines	0.225	30.00	13,792	No	No	No
Australia	0.216	30.00	15,944	Yes	Yes	Yes
South Africa	0.211	34.55	13,041	No	No	No
New Zealand	0.200	28.00	13,872	Yes	Yes	No
Germany	0.185	29.48	6,727	No	Yes	No
Chile	0.176	18.50	8,036	No	No	Yes
Japan	0.175	38.01	10,927	No	Yes	No
Venezuela	0.174	34.00	3,305	No	No	No
Malaysia	0.169	25.00	15,348	Yes	No	No
Israel	0.165	25.00	9,462	Yes	Yes	No
Brazil	0.164	34.00	6,773	No	No	No
Sweden	0.164	26.30	6,654	No	Yes	No
Argentina	0.154	35.00	8,363	No	No	No
Thailand	0.134	23.00	14,172	No	No	No
France	0.125	33.33	6,180	Yes	Yes	No
Italy	0.083	31.40	7,234	No	Yes	No
China	0.059	25.00	11,170	No	No	No
Saudi Arabia	0.056	20.00	10,866	No	Yes	No
Norway	0.054	28.00	6,248	No	Yes	No
India	0.045	32.45	12,068	Yes	No	No
Indonesia	0.032	25.00	16,355	No	No	No
Spain	0.109	30.00	6,103	No	Yes	No

Table 5: OLS Estimates of Model Coefficients

Dependent variable: U.S. royalties and license fees for asset a from country c in year t as a share of GDP, with imputations

Explanatory Variables	All Types Pooled	Industrial Processes	Software	Films	Trademarks
Log of Distance	-0.262	-0.266	-0.183	-0.291	-0.368
	(0.035)	(0.085)	(0.083)	(0.067)	(0.068)
Log of Corporate	-0.715	-2.136	-1.441	0.695	-2.047
Tax Rate	(0.123)	(0.349)	(0.318)	(0.246)	(0.301)
Economic Development	0.301	0.350	0.308	0.409	0.178
	(0.025)	(0.069)	(0.046)	(0.059)	(0.069)
Colonial Ties	0.324	0.280	0.524	0.357	0.044
	(0.051)	(0.138)	(0.109)	(0.104)	(0.123)
FTA with Intellectual	0.288	0.138	0.360	0.133	0.192
Property Provisions	(0.060)	(0.200)	(0.143)	(0.101)	(0.138)
Books	1.862				
	(0.111)				
Films	4.296				
	(0.105)				
Industrial Processes	5.092				
	(0.116)				
Trademarks	4.271				
	(0.112)				
Software	5.025				
	(0.105)				
Broadcasting	1.177				
	(0.110)				
Franchise Fees	3.255				
	(0.108)				
Constant	-5.982	-2.918	-2.543	-0.132	-1.745
	(0.341)	(0.752)	(0.728)	(0.606)	(0.622)
Number of observations	1,724	231	231	231	231
R^2 statistic	0.7758	0.3952	0.4588	0.3968	0.3512

Notes: Omitted asset type is "Other Intangibles." Robust standard errors are reported in parentheses.

16

Table 6: Country Index Values Based on the Econometric Model with Imputations

All Types of Assets Pooled Together

Countries	Point Estimate	95 % Confidence Interval	
Australia	2.56	2.14	2.89
Singapore	2.49	2.18	2.81
Canada	2.48	2.17	2.80
Ireland	2.16	1.87	2.44
France	2.12	1.84	2.40
United Kingdom	2.11	1.83	2.39
New Zealand	2.10	1.83	2.38
Israel	2.06	1.79	2.33
Norway	2.06	1.73	2.40
Switzerland	2.00	1.68	2.32
Korea	1.91	1.61	2.20
Sweden	1.89	1.58	2.19
Japan	1.84	1.54	2.13
Netherlands	1.83	1.54	2.13
Belgium	1.82	1.52	2.11
Germany	1.81	1.52	2.10
Chile	1.79	1.51	2.07
Hong Kong	1.76	1.48	2.05
Italy	1.74	1.46	2.02
Malaysia	1.71	1.49	1.93
Spain	1.69	1.42	1.96
Mexico	1.66	1.40	1.92
Saudi Arabia	1.65	1.39	1.92
Taiwan	1.59	1.33	1.84
Venezuela	1.45	1.22	1.68
Argentina	1.42	1.19	1.65
Brazil	1.41	1.19	1.64
South Africa	1.28	1.07	1.48
China	1.22	1.03	1.42
Thailand	1.19	1.00	1.38
India	1.13	1.00	1.28
Indonesia	1.07	0.89	1.24
Philippines	0.97	0.81	1.12

Note: The countries are sorted in descending order, based on the value of the point estimate.

Table 7: Country Index Values Based on the Econometric Model with Imputations

Countries	All Types Pooled	Industrial Processes	Software	Films	Trademarks
Australia	2.56	2.69	2.87	3.14	1.39
Singapore	2.49	2.60	2.80	3.04	1.34
Canada	2.48	2.60	2.80	3.03	1.34
Ireland	2.16	2.41	2.39	2.84	1.13
France	2.12	2.37	2.36	2.80	1.11
United Kingdom	2.11	2.35	2.34	2.78	1.10
New Zealand	2.10	2.35	2.34	2.77	1.09
Israel	2.06	2.30	2.30	2.71	1.07
Norway	2.06	2.40	2.11	2.80	1.22
Switzerland	2.00	2.32	2.04	2.71	1.18
Korea	1.91	2.02	2.01	2.33	1.15
Sweden	1.89	2.19	1.93	2.56	1.11
Japan	1.84	2.14	1.87	2.49	1.08
Netherlands	1.83	2.13	1.87	2.49	1.08
Belgium	1.82	2.11	1.85	2.46	1.07
Germany	1.81	2.10	1.85	2.46	1.07
Chile	1.79	1.88	1.89	2.17	1.08
Hong Kong	1.76	2.05	1.80	2.39	1.04
Italy	1.74	2.02	1.78	2.36	1.03
Malaysia	1.71	1.89	1.94	2.24	0.86
Spain	1.69	1.96	1.72	2.29	1.00
Mexico	1.66	1.74	1.77	2.00	1.00
Saudi Arabia	1.65	1.92	1.69	2.24	0.97
Taiwan	1.59	1.85	1.62	2.15	0.94
Venezuela	1.45	1.69	1.48	1.97	0.86
Argentina	1.42	1.65	1.45	1.92	0.84
Brazil	1.41	1.64	1.44	1.92	0.83
South Africa	1.28	1.49	1.31	1.74	0.75
China	1.22	1.42	1.25	1.66	0.72
Thailand	1.19	1.38	1.21	1.61	0.70
India	1.13	1.22	1.34	1.45	0.52
Indonesia	1.06	1.24	1.09	1.44	0.63
Philippines	0.97	1.13	0.99	1.31	0.57

Note: The countries are sorted in descending order, based on the value of the All Types index.

Table 8: Alternative Econometric Techniques

Dependent variable: U.S. royalty of royalties and license fees for all types of asset from country c in year t as a share of GDP, with imputations

Explanatory Variables	OLS Model	Poisson Model
Log of Distance	-0.262	-0.307
	(0.035)	(0.060)
Log of Corporate Tax Rate	-0.715	-2.792
	(0.123)	(0.111)
Economic Development	0.301	0.390
	(0.025)	(0.051)
Colonial Ties	0.324	0.509
	(0.051)	(0.089)
FTA with Intellectual Property Provisions	0.288	-0.051
	(0.060)	(0.101)
Books	1.862	2.315
	(0.111)	(0.203)
Films	4.296	4.646
	(0.105)	(0.230)
Industrial Processes	5.092	6.160
	(0.116)	(0.193)
Trademarks	4.271	5.081
	(0.112)	(0.203)
Software	5.025	6.002
	(0.105)	(0.203)
Broadcasting	1.177	1.523
	(0.110)	(0.228)
Franchise Fees	3.255	3.578
	(0.108)	(0.232)
Constant	-5.982	-9.338
	(0.341)	(0.678)
Number of observations	1,724	1,848

Notes: Omitted asset type is "Other Intangibles." Robust standard errors are reported in parentheses.

Table 9: Country Index Values for Alternative Econometric Estimators

Countries	OLS Model	Poisson Model
Australia	2.56	2.98
Singapore	2.49	2.89
Canada	2.48	2.88
Ireland	2.16	2.88
France	2.12	2.84
United Kingdom	2.11	2.82
New Zealand	2.10	2.81
Israel	2.06	2.76
Norway	2.06	2.67
Switzerland	2.00	2.59
Sweden	1.91	2.04
Japan	1.89	2.44
Netherlands	1.84	2.38
Belgium	1.83	2.37
Germany	1.82	2.35
Hong Kong	1.81	2.34
Malaysia	1.79	1.89
Italy	1.76	2.28
Spain	1.74	2.25
Saudi Arabia	1.71	2.30
Korea	1.69	2.18
Taiwan	1.66	1.73
Chile	1.65	2.14
Venezuela	1.59	2.06
Argentina	1.45	1.88
Brazil	1.42	1.83
Mexico	1.41	1.83
South Africa	1.28	1.66
China	1.22	1.58
Thailand	1.19	1.54
India	1.13	1.55
Indonesia	1.06	1.38
Philippines	0.97	1.25

Table 10: Alternative Econometric Estimators

Dependent variable: U.S. receipts of royalties and license fees for all types of asset from country c in year t as a share of GDP, with imputations

Explanatory Variables	OLS Model with Imputations	OLS Model without Imputations	Adds Year Fixed Effects
Log of Distance	-0.262	-0.256	-0.262
	(0.035)	(0.035)	(0.035)
Log of Corporate Tax Rate	-0.715	-0.598	-0.729
	(0.123)	(0.126)	(0.125)
Economic Development	0.301	0.303	0.303
	(0.025)	(0.025)	(0.025)
Colonial Ties	0.324	0.323	0.323
	(0.051)	(0.052)	(0.051)
FTA with Intellectual Property Provisions	0.288	0.277	0.285
	(0.060)	(0.060)	(0.060)
Books	1.862	1.945	1.860
	(0.111)	(0.119)	(0.111)
Films	4.296	4.408	4.293
	(0.105)	(0.112)	(0.105)
Industrial Processes	5.092	5.205	5.089
	(0.116)	(0.123)	(0.116)
Trademarks	4.271	4.364	4.268
	(0.112)	(0.118)	(0.111)
Software	5.025	5.259	5.202
	(0.105)	(0.111)	(0.105)
Broadcasting	1.177	1.174	1.174
	(0.110)	(0.122)	(0.110)
Franchise Fees	3.255	3.286	3.252
	(0.108)	(0.115)	(0.108)
Constant	-5.982	-6.025	-5.939
	(0.341)	(0.338)	(0.342)
Number of observations	1,724	1,595	1,724
R-squared statistic	0.7758	0.7801	0.7764

Notes: Omitted asset type is "Other Intangibles." Robust standard errors are reported in parentheses.

Table 11: Spearman Rank Correlations for the Indices

	WEF Index	Park Index	BSA Non-Piracy Rate*
Indices in the Literature			
WEF Index	1.00		
Park Index	0.50	1.00	
BSA Non-Piracy Rate*	0.81	0.62	1.00
Index Based on the OLS Models with Imputation			
All Types of Assets	0.74	0.60	0.77
Industrial Processes	0.78	0.59	0.81
Software	0.70	0.52	0.71
Films	0.78	0.59	0.80
Trademarks	0.71	0.51	0.75
Index Based on the Poisson Model with Imputation			
All Types of Assets	0.78	0.56	0.80
Index Based on the OLS Model without Imputation			
All Types of Assets	0.74	0.60	0.77

(*) Note: This is equal to 100 minus the BSA piracy rate, divided by 100.